Loren's Musings

Dr. Loren Siffring

Table of Contents

Loren's Musings

I. Musings about Life

Be a Man to Follow

His smile is as wide as the man is tall,
      And his heart is easily that immense.
The love of Christ that flows from his eyes
      Shows his love for Jesus is that intense.

He's a husband, a father and businessman too.
      Wherever he goes, his mission is clear.
He seeks Godly wisdom which sets his course;
      The words of "The Book" are held dear.

He seeks to prophesy in all that he says;
      His influence causes his hearers to grow.
The "Unity of the Spirit" he strives to preserve;
      He'll show you the path so you'll know.

The problems he tackles are all down to earth.
      "Good gift answers" all come from above.
One who follows his example surely will find
      That his heart is wrapped up in God's love.

So the follower becomes the leader of men;
      The peace of the Lord is his guide.
If you search for his source, you'll find it for sure:
      No "genuine seeker" is ever denied.

Maturity

What is meant by the word maturity? The bible tells us that things can be seen first in the natural and then in the spiritual realm. (1Cor.15:46)

In the natural realm a plant is considered mature when it is able to reproduce itself. A seed is mature when it has developed to the point when, if properly positioned and cared for, will grow into the same kind of a plant from which it came.

It is true that some will reproduce in different degrees of increase. Some will produce 30, some 60 and some 100 fold.

Sexual maturity is attained when the egg or sperm is capable of combining to produce offspring.

We all are thrilled as we see increasing maturity in those who are attaining abilities in talking, walking, caring for self and making right, safe choices.

Time alone does not automatically produce maturity. Parents, teachers, mentors, fellow travelers and trials and errors may be involved in the process of coming to maturity.

The writer of Hebrews states that we should go on to maturity, not remaining babes, leaving the foundational teachings in order to assist others in their maturing process. (Hebrews 5:12-6:12)

The two great teachers to help in our process of obtaining godly maturity are The Word of God and The Spirit of God. Paul when writing to the Philippians says that a sign of maturity is expressed in pressing on toward the prize of the upward call of God in Christ Jesus. (Phil.3:12-16) When writing to the Corinthian believers, he encourages them to become mature in their understanding, being aided by the Holy Spirit. (1 Cor.14:20)

Whatever God instructs us to do, we can be confident that he will provide for us all that it takes to accomplish the task. We, however, should be asking that these things would be coming to us so that we can be obedient in carrying out His will in our lives.

Success

To laugh often and much
To win the respect of intelligent people
and the affection of children
To earn the appreciation of honest critics
and endure the betrayal of false friends
To appreciate beauty
To find the best in others
To leave the world a bit better, weather a healthy
child,
a garden patch or a redeemed social condition
To know even one life has breathed easier
because you have lived:
This is to have succeeded.
N.B.

Creativity and Inspiration

I believe that creativity should not be limited to inventors or persons involved in the visual or performing arts.

The first statement in the Bible about God is that He is a creator, and since mankind was created by Him and in His image, we are all innately, creative.

Every action or word creates something that was not previously seen or experienced.

Some things that are created are basically destructive or chaotic, while others bring new vision, harmony or beauty. I want to create the latter.

Inspiration is a gift, freely given to us. As the gift is given, we become the steward of it and have the responsibility to care for it.

Satisfaction and pleasure for me comes from trying to express the verve of life and the unending variety in everything that I see around me.

Even though a piece is not rendered perfectly, when a viewer becomes a participant in the presentation and can identify with some part of it, I am encouraged.

My aim and hope is that anything that I do will ultimately bring Glory to God, and when it does, I become fully alive.

Forces of Change

I'm watching now, at the edge of water,
As each new wave patterns the sand.
The movements, it seems, are nearly the same
Yet, ever new etchings are left on the land.

Some of the new-made marks are subtle
Remembering, I say "I've seen that before"
But, looking more closely, I see they are special;
I see the distinctions are there more and more.

Trials and storms all leave their patterns:
Some beautifully jagged, some smooth as glass.
The results are a story of tests that have happened:
Some marks will remain while others will pass.

Most parts of our lives resemble the beaches,
New patterns theron, inscribed day by day
Not only the weather, but numerous circumstances
Most are transient, but some come to stay.

The most important to us are the changes
  Made as people in our lives come, stay, or go.
Some marks are temporary, some stay forever,
  Some stimulate us to change and to grow.

Clear results are evident in each of our lives
  As close family and friends, there at the ready
Like the wind or the water to wash away loose stuff
  Revealing the rocks, which below, make us steady

No use of protecting ourselves from the forces
  Of persons and trials and events that are sent
The final product is, of course, God's design
  Showing the way that our lives should be spent.

The choice will be ours as to how we'll respond
  As the winds and the waves come our way.
How will we take it when words come from someone
  Which cause us to alter our plans for the day?

We are changed by the lives we encounter
  So we, like the beaches, are taking new form.
We are the sum total of all interactions.
  What we are, is the landscape after the storms.

Guard Your Lips

As you walk through your days, you have chances galore.
　　When you are with folks who have needs
To give what you have to fill in their gaps,
　　They will often remember your deeds.

Sometimes it will be that the things that you give
　　Are not goods, but a promise you make.
This two-part gift will be measured, for sure
　　Is your follow-through truth or a fake?

When you've given your word, it may cause you some hurt
　　To deliver the goods like you spoke.
It will measure you, man, so be careful to speak
　　"Your word is your bond"　That's no joke!

The best gift you can give to a wife, son or daughter
　　Is a promise that's kept, like it's spoken.
A wall is produced that is hard to remove
　　Whenever a promise is broken.

To be 'quick to hear' and 'slow to speak'
　　Will determine the words that come out.
Once spoken, the fruit that they bear will be seen
　　To produce life, love and light, but not doubt.

11

Process - Yarn To Sweater

Starting as single threads- many tiny ones –
Part organic part chemical combinations

Twisted and joined into uniform strands
Colored together, now uniform, but each dye lot different,
Prepared in loose skeins and offered for use.

Beautiful yarn, soft, what now? – what else?

We need a vision – a plan – a pattern – many choices,
From stuff to function – there are many steps.

Trials, repeats, dropped stitches, then repairs –
Decipher the directions, measure, count again-

After application of skill, care and work,
A beautiful product begins to emerge.

Impatience is overcome because of the visualized goal –

The hopes and desires become a reality as
The parts are finished and joined. Celebrate!

How like our lives is this awesome, involved process

Gifts, talents, preferences, times of pain and growth
Produce a skein, ready to be fashioned into a service unit

Different directions, perhaps some even wrong,
Impatience, wandering, dropped stitches, then repair –

All toward the end that only God can see.

Amazing that He cares so specifically for each part

That He lets the final result be just right,

Only then can we begin to see what was produced

And have the many "whys" explained.

Grand is Hard to Beat

What makes something worthy of the designation
"Grand"?

Must it be a canyon or a canal or a finale?

The most important and universal one gets attached to
parent.

Here the title comes, not because of something you do;
      It is just that one of your progeny couples up and a
      Grandchild becomes center stage.

You get all of the credit and all of the bragging rights.

> It is somewhat like saying "we won" when a sports
> team of your liking defeats a worthy opponent.
> You didn't contribute a thing, save perhaps a vocal shout,
> and yet – victory is claimed as if you did it.

So, taking the credit; you exclaim – "What a wonderful,
unique, exceptional, intelligent, beautiful Grandchild"

Of course, all of the above is true – and perhaps there isn't
A better word that would describe it than GRAND.

So – in answer to your inquiry about My Grandchildren –

> (I'm sure you must have asked, or were about too,
> for who wouldn't be eager to hear?)

It is true – they are all GRAND

Each one, a never before known combination of gifts,
attributes and potential, just waiting to be released.

And here is the special part – For the Grand parent
Because they are grand to you and you are grand to them,
you are positioned to encourage, praise, instruct and
share things and stories from the treasure chest that
time has given to you

You can help them appreciate their uniqueness and the
     correspondent responsibilities which will take them
     from one grand opportunity to the next.

Every situation can make one bitter or better –
     A Grandparent can help a Grandchild make the right
     choice which can turn each event into usable currency
     and also discover the proper time to spend it.

What value could be given to this grand-to-grand
     relationship? There is nothing at all to which
     it can be compared. Just receive it as great!

Don't waste precious time and energy trying to buy, bribe
     or demand this place – it is always a "given".

Give, therefore, what you have – yourself – be available.

Listen to their voices and their hearts speaking.

While this grand drama has center stage, enter in –
     relax – Have a great show!

Let God show you the Grand Finale!

It is broader than the Grand Canal

More beautiful and varied than the Grand Canyon

It is the ultimate Grand Gift!

Awakened to Greet Life

The rousing repetitive notes of the alarm transfer me
From the all consuming dream to the reality of
anticipation,
Knowing that in less than one hour my friend will join me
For a few hours, for an exchange of deeds, hopes and
dreams.

Is it the welcoming smile, the embrace, or the sound of
his voice
That brings such fulfillment? Where do these sensations
originate?
Where do they reside? Is it all chemical reaction, electric
potential
At the cellular level, or does it consist of unseen forces?

Is it akin to gravity or magnetic fields this drawing
together?
What medium can I use to express the joy that is here?
Perhaps musical notes or a physical dance will do.
Togetherness is like a needed drink of water.

Friendship is a full meal, with texture, and a blend of
flavors
Providing more than just enough nourishment to survive,
Placing a deposit which will energize, plus more to give
away.
I'm wide awake now, ready to enjoy my friend.

Hand Held

Here is a safe place that provides welcome and promise
Of health, despite the problems of the journey.
Specific steps are demonstrated and delineated
As healing comes through the hands.

Tender, sensitive, firm and calloused, ready for the job
Changing, yet remaining the same, ushering in a mystery.
How could the same hands, tear down and build up?
The answer must be outside natural forces.

These are the same hands that comforted me at a time
Of loss, giving me courage to go on,
Providing both direction and the energy necessary
When both seemed inadequate or lacking altogether.

Was it a dream, or was it real? I was falling
With no solid place to land.
The end of it all was the reassuring pressure on me
That comes from the strength of His hands.

It is new and fresh to me to see that
These are the same hands that were used
To strongly correct me when the boundaries
Had been stretched or traversed.

My turn comes to reach out and touch another
After I have welcomed the strong hand given me.

What a joy it is to be in the continuum
Providing strength, correction, hope and connection
To His strong hands.

Where is the Point?

Being the "point-man" has such appeal
You're out there in front, on display,
Dealing with problems, seeking the truth,
Significant work for each day.

One might believe that climbing up
And attaining a place at the top
Is worth stepping on others, even friends
That nothing should cause you to stop.

Perhaps you think that success will be yours
When you're on the top, looking down
Being adored by everyone else
As the highest one in the town.

Accolades numerous, many folks giving praise
Are the perks so many strive for.
That reward is short-lived and soon fades away
You will then be looking for more.

When you realize that isn't the way
You'll find the door to real peace,

"Abundant Life" is promised to you
    In service you'll find that release

Before time began, it was in the Lord's mind
    The role and the place you should fill.
Where service awaits you, fulfillment is yours
His glory is shown, if you will.

Temporal satisfaction is its own reward
    For it, no heavenly treasure is stored.
The rewards come now, or later, - your choice
    The promised, clear word from the Lord.

God's leadership pyramid's point is down
    All the weight is supported from there.
The Lord as our cornerstone, takes the abuse
    He's promised our troubles to bear.

Servanthood starts as a place of support
    Then what is above can expand
The point taking on the additional weight
    For this is the way God has planned.

The one who is chosen to be a "point-man"
    Must willingly receive more load
In order that others become more equipped
    To follow and find the right road.

Our Lord, as a servant, while washing the feet
    Of the ones He was training to lead
Said "you now, do likewise and you will do well
    "With compassion for all, you'll proceed".

To let gifts from God be freely outpoured
    We need His support and His care
Expanding so all can give love away
    To stand and avoid Satan's snare.

So when, as a "point-man", you're standing secure
    On the Rock that is solid, Our Lord,
Then you'll support those who want to be used
    As His Love is being outpoured.

Abide With Me

Abide with me! Fast fall the eventide;
The darkness deepens; Lord, with me abide.
When other helpers fail and comforts flee,
Help of the helpless, oh, abide with me.

Swift to its close ebbs out life's little day;
Earth's joys grow dim, its glories pass away;
Change and decay in all around I see.
O Thou, who changest not, abide with me!

I need Thy presence every passing hour;
What but Thy grace can foil the tempter's power?
Who like Thyself my guide and stay can be?
Through cloud and sunshine, oh, abide with me!

II. Special Occasions

Ode to a King

Hark! Listen up! Lend me your ear!
    You don't want to miss what I'm saying here

God's allotted years are three score and ten
    What a great life these seventy years have been

For a man who's a king in everyone's eyes
    Though he needs not a crown, nor any disguise.

It's hard to describe him, except he's the best.
    He welcomes and listens and fixes with zest.

So here's to our friend – that jolly good fellow
    Instead of just aging, he's becoming more mellow.

May God as your source keep giving you grace
    We're always delighted by the smile on your face.

Fifty is Nifty

We've come to the party so let the cork pop
    He made it to fifty, he's not ready to stop;

Though he gave up his youth, he still looks like a child
    When he enters a game his system goes wild.

Although it is dangerous, he says "just watch me"
    Then he strains his whole body, his shoulder or knee.

We're all glad that his mind is still growing stronger;
    He tackles a problem, gets it started, lasts longer.

He's a disciple of Jesus, his Savior and Lord
    As he has followed His lead, he has never been bored.

You will never find a more affable guy;
    He's a joy to be joined to whenever you try.

Your wife has a mate who's above all the rest,
    And your son hit the jackpot: a father who is best.

If I look in the dictionary for the meaning of friend,
    I'll find pictures of you from the start to the end.

He'd give the shirt off his back; I say "don't take it."
    The sleeves are too long, in the middle I'd break it.

We can follow the example of a life that's well led,
    Be encouraged and challenged by what he has said.

We're glad to be here and to help celebrate
    With this man of God, servant, friend, father and mate.

We Celebrate You

With you, we celebrate that you came
    To the end of another great year!
We should send gifts to your mother who endured
    The labor of bringing you here.

Your smile and your zest for this life
    Encourages each person around
Your charming accent adds value indeed
    Causing hope and joy to abound.

So fly the balloons and shoot fire-works and
    Wave banners which will help us to say
"We're glad that you're part of our lives
    As we wish you this HAPPY BIRTHDAY!"

At Her Half Way Point

Hail to you who wears many hats, of wife, mother
    And friend who gets things done.
She's also an artist and chauffer, so we call her
    The woman of Proverbs Thirty-One.

She's content in what state she's in,
    Be it in Michigan or in Texas.
She's thrilled that a car still gets her there
    Whether it's a Chevette or a Lexus.

Her permanent attitude is "Life is a blast!"
    She's always creative in getting things done.
Her choice is the present, not future or past;
    She even makes work look like fun.

Some say "Fifty is nifty" and we sure agree
    Like, wine, cheese and very good art
The 'ever young' fits this to a tee.
    She's great, getting better, loving life is her part.

At Three Score

The best ahead and Sixty, indeed,
You're on the right track and you're gaining speed.

All of the work and distress from before
Have produced the keys to the open door.

For all that's ahead, the battles to fight,
As you put on your armor and walk in the light,

Respond to His leading, while using your gifting
To speak out with clarity, clearly uplifting

All who desire to hear God and find
How to respond fully with heart, strength and mind.

After you've done all, faithfully stand
And see what the Lord will put in your hand.

Your intimacy with the Father, others will see
Your dependence on Him, where He wants each to be.

In your confidence in Him, you'll be able to rest;
God uses those whose yielding is best

For in your meekness, His strength will show
That all good gifts come from above to below
Shepherd the flock as it's given to you
To challenge, and to love, and to sacrifice, too.

A Thanksgiving Day

Should I only be thankful on one day each year
      When I'm gathered with loved ones at a bounteous meal?
Why not let my thanksgivings establish each thought
      And see each moment as a gift that is real?

Must I wait for the anniversary of a past event
      Only then celebrate with the person I love?
For the great marker-points in my journey of life
      I can daily be grateful for this gift from above.

My birthday arrives on the same date each year
      Reminding me of the life gift that is mine
This day and all others give reason to shout
      "It's time to rejoice – this day is divine".

Why do I think I must wait for the date
      For a calendar number, before I rejoice?
Can't I, right now, decide and make up my mind
      To daily let thankfulness be my first choice?

It's settled! I'll do it! On each day that I'm given
      No delay, starting now 'till the last beat of my heart
I'll remember the blessings that have all come to me
      Not assigning just one day for doing my part.

Nine Eleven, O One

It was on a Tuesday morning
Four years ago on this date
That terror struck and caused us to see
That evil is at our gate

We banded together and prayed
"God show us what we should do
Not just for a day, but from now on
To show that our trust is in You"

We saw that the bravery of men
Gave help at the cost of their lives
Compassion poured out for the loss
Of parents, friends, husbands and wives.

The fact that we're all in a war
Satan's plans becoming more clear
Should cause us to trust even more
In our Lord and make us draw near.

But alas, many want to place blame
And hope war will soon pass away
Now knowing that hearts must be changed
And evil be routed each day.

The place where terror is born
Must be taken and freedom come there
The cost of this duty is high
Already many have given their share.
The suffering is great, but we can rejoice
In knowing that God is in charge.
We need to respond with all that we have
Letting the likeness of Jesus enlarge.

III. Seasons

Through Other's Eyes

Things that are dulled by being familiar
      Take on a new luster when viewed new this day
Through eyes newly here from a distant land
      Help me refresh and see clearly his way.

Explaining to another can cause me to think
      Just what are my reasons to celebrate so
Energize my thankfulness, sharpen my view
      When seen through the eyes that are newly aglow.

Why Christmas lights? Why fresh greenery?
      Why is it right to search day and night
To find the gift that is 'just the one', perfect!
      Causing eyes to reveal that it now brings delight.

Unless I can see through the eyes of a child
      Observe through his heart, what would give him a lift
Then I could share in his great expectation
      As he waits for the day for receiving a gift.

Though my eyesight is fine, and I'm glad I can see
      I will see more as my vision expands.
My world is enlarged as I take in your view
      Exceeding by far what I held in my plans.

An elderly sage, whose eyes record history
      Can give a perspective, so different from now
Expanding compassion and depth I'd not seen
      To view the present, he'll show us just how

What a joy and a gift to have compound eyes
> To share in what others observed.
My world is expanding and I can enjoy
> More than I, by myself, have deserved.

To us, in His word, God has made clear His plan
> Of how to see His gifts, and all things provided
This Godly perspective is so rich and full
> That we are always expanded, excited.

Reflections on Early Fall

The fall of each year is a time of harvest, seeing the fruit of labor. Seed is harvested which will ensure future crops. Food is preserved for the less productive months ahead.

It is also a time of refocusing, a time of renewal and a preparation time for the upcoming year.

Visual images abound. Just try to explain the vivid colors of Autumn and you quickly realize that language is not up to the task. On a clear, crisp day, the light of the sun illuminating the magnificent spectrum of colors and textures of the leaves, stems and fruit, creates sights which are more than a little difficult to express. Being at a loss, we just blurt our "come see for yourself." Or "here is a photo that I took to capture a moment, but it fails to do justice to the sights that I saw."

Visual images have a profound and lasting effect upon us and evoke various emotions.

One dark blot on this marvelously changing landscape (at least throughout the month of October), is the concentration of fear producing things, celebrating death, violence and horror. This preoccupation seems to be growing in popularity each time this season rolls around. We are encouraged to witness gore, and adrenalin producing surprises as entertainment, seemingly not realizing that the images and emotional responses become residual in our memories and cause unhealthy emotional and physical responses. Compartmentalized thinking seems to be able to isolate this activity from all of the rest of life, saying "it's all just in fun, great fun."

Any person who does not participate in these activities is labeled as a killjoy or a legalist.

No one knows the collective effect of this repeated process, but it is well known that the effect is magnified in children. Before the age of five years, children cannot distinguish between fantasy and reality. Repeated exposure of even cartoons like the Roadrunner and the Coyote which depict the characters killing one another and springing back to life promote rage and acting out without seeing the consequences of injuring or pain to one another. A child donning a Superman cape is convinced that he can fly if he dives off the loft banister.

Just when parents are trying to instill in their children the value of kindness and service, a mixed message comes when they are encouraged to dress up and then go door-to-door demanding treats be given to them or else tricks (i.e. vandalism) will result.

It is true that children love to dress up, but that can be a part of their regular play time, not associated only with the celebration of the dark side of this one night which has been claimed by many to be Satan's own.

If we want to concentrate and meditate on whatever things are true, noble, just, pure, lovely and of good report or are praiseworthy or have virtue, we should consider our focus and involvement with these sights and events which decrease the beauty of this season.

Symbols of Sacrifice

The sky is filled with color: red and green and blue
    Bursts of gold and silver illuminate dark night.
We experience here a transient beauty,
    But nothing of real value came without a fight.

The rockets red glare, the bombs bursting in air
    Each year a reminder of our freedom and its cost.
Yes, we desire victory; can it come without the pain,
    Could everyone agree to peace, with no lives lost?

Loren's Musings

Is it proper for us all to sit and be amazed
    In such a fashion, with a simulated clash?
To ohh and ahh and make our comments on
    The loudness of the bang or brightness of the flash?

If, in fact, this grand display can help us
    Focus on the willing price, once paid by men,
Then let us enter into it with gusto
    And be, at end, more grateful than we've been.

A parallel exists when thinking of the cross.
    We often see it represented clean and pure
As jewelry or a building decoration
    Not as a cruel means of bringing death for sure.

We see, when empty, the place where His love saved us
    From the fate that would be ours upon the cross.
The value of this gift is beyond measure;
    It transfers to us His bounty, not our loss.

So view the sky alive with brightness, light and sound
    And see the rugged cross, now empty for our sake
Remember those who gave up life to bring us freedom
    Their sacrifice brings life for us to take.

It's Spring

Myriad shades of green emerge
Bursting out of a disguise of being dead.

The alchemy of lead to gold does not begin to thrill me
As much as this grey to green eruption.

New life appearing brings a deep excitation of hope and
An increased awareness of connection to the source of all life.

The numberless brilliant facets of this re-occurring gem
Are everywhere revealed, exciting and tantalizing all our senses

Mostly familiar colors, but unexpectedly fresh and new,
Textures and odors penetrate our beings and lift us upward.

We marvel that we've been given organs of identification
To receive, absorb and integrate this burst of newness

With memories of past times, this, the promised season.
Spring, a time to receive the gift, exult in it, and share it.

IV. Be What You Can Be

Be What You Can Be
~Charles DeHeart

This vast land of rich abundance
Nurtures those who would be free
Beckons to earth's striving people;
"Come! Be what you can be."

Refrain:
We the people love this land where
Freedom lets our spirit soar.
Let us guard, protect our nation
For the future evermore.

Cherished laws provide the framework
That secures our liberty.
Laws consented, not decreed say
"Now! Be what you can be."

Refrain:
Mighty strength restrains aggressors,
Rushes aid where there is need.
Spreads the message by example, "All
Should be what they can be."

V. Thoughts about the Scriptures

God's Shopping List For Us

As we read the Proverbs, we are told to pay less attention to gold, silver and precious stones and fix our attention upon getting four things which have greater value.

In the natural, every shopping list would probably contain certain basics and some extras.

So what are the basics we are told to get?

They are:
Wisdom
Understanding
Knowledge &
Instruction

The reference to the value of these are listed in the following places in The Proverbs:
Proverbs: 3:13, Chapters 4 & 5,
Prov.8:9,10,33   16:16,22
Prov.:19:8,27   23:12   24:3

How are these characteristics distinct and how do they differ?

Let's begin with KNOWLEDGE:

Knowledge(science) is the awareness of facts. These are apprehended by our senses: things we have seen, heard,touched, or sm elled.

Then we come to UNDERSTANDING:

Understanding is the comprehension of the meaning and interrelationships of the facts that we have obtained.

Then WISDOM

GOD'S Word reveals to us that the fear of the Lord is the beginning of wisdom. God's wisdom reveals God's purposes. It is as we regard, with awe and respect, God's person, that we are able to see and align ourselves with His Heart and purposes for our lives.

And INSTRUCTION:

Instruction, therefore is the availability to us of any of the above being realized by one person and passed on to another: the ability to convey to someone else is 'good advice'.

Proverbs 24:3 helps us understand this process: "Through wisdom a house is built, through understanding it is established and through knowledge its rooms are filled with rare and beautiful treasures."

The Word of God treats man as tripartite. Each of us is a created Spirit, dwelling in a Soul and living in a Body.

Knowledge, Understanding and Wisdom come to us via the three different parts of our beings:

KNOWLEDGE (awareness of facts - bits of information) are received by our various senses in our BODIES.

UNDERSTANDING (comprehension of meaning and interrelationships of and usages of facts) takes place in our mind, which is one of the three parts of our SOUL. The other two parts, our emotions (feelings) and our will are closely associated in this process.

WISDOM (God's purposes) comes to us via the portion of our SPIRIT which receives revelation from God (intuition). The other two parts of our spirit are conscience and worship (communion).

1Thessalonians 5:23 states: "May the God of peace himself sanctify you wholly; and may your spirit and soul and body be kept sound and blameless at the

coming of our Lord Jesus Christ."

When we set out to get these vital things on our 'shopping list', we must be sure that they are aligned with the standards of the Word of God because:

1.There is available to us worldly wisdom as well as Godly or Spiritual wisdom.

1Corinthians 3:19 "The wisdom of this world is foolishness to God.
James 1:5 "If any of you lacks wisdom, he should ask God, who gives generously to all without finding fault, and it will be given to him,"

2.If we seek knowledge alone, on our own, we can become puffed up by it or begin to believe that we 'have it all' when we really only have a portion.

3.We can become the victims of <u>mis-</u>understandings or <u>erroneous</u>-understandings. - and

4.We can be in difficulty if we obtain instruction from others which does not square with clear Biblical truth.

Will we be perfect in our shopping trip
as we involve ourselves in getting the things which are more
valuable than gold, silver and precious stones?

Probably not!

However, we should always be in the process.

Let's bring back the promised valuable items.

Praise

Sometimes it is difficult to receive a compliment without
wanting to adjust the other persons perspective of the situation. Yet,
the bible tells us to: "Let others praise you and not you yourselves"
Proverbs 27:2. This is difficult because we all have desires of hearing
good things about ourselves and at the same time we have fears of
becoming proud or of being manipulated by another's words. The
problem may be that we are so aware of the condition of our own
impure hearts that we may not have hope for change.

Jeremiah 9:10 (Amp) says: "The heart is deceitful above
all things and it is exceedingly perverse and corrupt and severely,
mortally sick! Who can know it (perceive, understand, be acquainted
with his own heart and mind)? I, The Lord, search the mind, I try the
heart, even to give to every man, according to his ways, according to
the fruit of his doing." Because of God's love for us: accepting us
just as we are, yet changing us to become just like Jesus, what does he

use? In our natural world, heat is used for removing impurities.

Two parallel passages in the book of Proverbs help us understand this process and the desired result.

Proverbs 27:3   The crucible for silver
the furnace for gold,
but the Lord tests the heart.

Proverbs 27:21   The crucible for silver
the furnace for gold,
but man is tested by
the praise he receives
(or – a man is valued by
what others say of him)

When silver is placed in a crucible, heat is applied to the bottom and the impurities, known as dross, rise to the top and can be scooped off and disposed. Increasing the heat will further purify, causing other impurities to rise to the top to be removed. The silver is considered pure when no more dross comes to the surface.

Gold, however, must receive its purifying heat, not only from the bottom, but also from the sides, and from above; hence the use of the use of the refiners fire, as a furnace. When gold is heated in a furnace, the impurities rise to the surface and are vaporized.

The silversmith is satisfied that the silver is pure when he observes no more dross.

The goldsmith removes the container of gold from the furnace and observes the surface. If the gold has been purified, the surface is a perfect mirror, reflecting the image of the goldsmith. If the reflection is at all cloudy, the gold is returned to the inside of the furnace for more heat until the reflected image is perfectly clear. When God looks into our hearts, He wants to see a clear reflection of Himself; the process is to continually purify us to make us more like Jesus.

Proverbs 27:21 in the Amplified Bible helps us see how the Lord uses the praises of others to purify the heart: "As the refining pot for silver and the furnace for gold (bring forth all of the impurities of the metal) so let a man be in his trial of praise (ridding it of all that is base or insincere) -- for a man is judged by what he praises and of what he boasts."

Psalms 12:6: "The words of the Lord are pure like silver, tried in a furnace of earth, purified seven times." David cried out: "Examine me and prove me: test my heart and mind." Psalm 26:2.

God does use others to help us in this process. "As iron sharpens iron, so one man sharpens another." Proverbs 27:17. Praise is not the final measure of one's worth. Our worth has been established by the price paid for our redemption.

So there we have it: God uses the purifying property of the praises of others to purify our hearts. How praise is received can be used by God in the purifying process of our hearts, removing the

impurities of manipulation and pride. If whatever we have been given is of value to another as it is passed on without additions or subtractions, we can receive the praise and acknowledge that it is a good gift from God. Giving thanks to God for the gift of that praise which comes from others, gives the glory back to God.

The prophet Malachi speaks of the coming of our Lord (Malachi 3:2,3): "Who can endure the day of his coming? ... He is like a refiner's fire ... He will set as a refiner and purifier of silver. He will purify the priests... and refine them like gold and silver, that they may offer to the Lord, offerings in righteousness." We can resist the heat that God uses to refine us, but that may only prolong the process. This may be a slow, long, uncomfortable journey. It seems best to give up our control and freely submit to the process which has been ordered by The Father who loves us.

"Beloved, do not think it strange concerning the fiery trial which is taking place to test your quality... but rejoice." I Peter 4:12

I AM

When asked, "Who are you," what is my first response? Is it "I am a child of God," or "A follower of Jesus Christ"? Do you immediately think, "I am a light or a door or a good shepherd, etc."? Or do I respond with: my name or my occupation or my natural relationships.

When Jesus was confronted in the garden where his betrayer led the soldiers of the High Priest, He said "Whom do you seek?" When they replied, "Jesus of Nazareth, he said, "I AM," John 18: 4-6

I AM was and is the definitive identification, which God has given to mankind. It was the answer to Moses' question, "Whom shall I say has sent me to deliver the people from the bondage of Egypt?"

I AM is the title God gives himself, meaning that He is eternally self existent and that He will be to all people whatever they would ever need Him to be.

All devout Jews (including these soldiers who were sent to capture him) looked forward to the coming of the Messiah. He would proclaim that he was the "I AM."

When this was spoken in the garden, the result was that the captors fell backwards to the ground. This was not a show of their power. In fact, it was a dangerous act, since they were carrying weapons and torches. In modern vernacular, we would say that:

"they were blown away!"

Did the Holy Spirit cause them to be slain or cause them to recall the promise of the returning I AM? After they recovered, they witnessed God's healing power when the severed ear of Malcus was restored.

Then Jesus said "Let these others go their way, you may take me".

Earlier in his gospel, John had recorded Jesus proclaiming seven times that he was the, I AM in specific areas.

6:35   I AM the bread of life
8:12   I AM the light of the world
10:9   I AM the door
10:11 I AM the good shepherd
11:25 I AM the resurrection and the life
14:6   I AM the way, the truth and the life
(to, about, and of the Father)
15:1   I AM the true vine

Each of these statements stands alone. However, their sequence may well have significance as well:

He is the bread, giving life and sustenance
He is the light, showing the way to walk
He is the door to life temporal and eternal
He is the good shepherd, giving guidance and protection
He is the resurrection and the life, conquering death and providing ongoing relationship

He is the way to the Father, the truth about the Father and the life of the Father

He is the true vine, providing fruitfulness to all who will abide in him.

Before his death, resurrection and departure Jesus said, "While I am in the world, I am the light. After I go away, you are the light of the world" Matthew 5:14

Since Christ lives in us by the power of the Holy Spirit (Galatians 2:20), could it be that our identification is established by Him so that we might represent Him in the other ways that Jesus declared that He was on earth?

For a person walking in darkness, can I be the light that leads him to Christ, the true light?

For another person, could I be the door to open the way for him to come to find Christ as his Lord?

Am I willing to be a good shepherd to protect and care for those given to me (i.e. as a spouse, parent or mentor)?

Do I know and can I show the way to the Father, the truth about the Father and the life of the Father?

Is my identification "one who is abiding in the true vine" so that I can provide encouragement toward fruitfulness for someone else? He has his Wisdom (i.e. His Purpose) to give to all who would

look to Him and rely upon Him.

Apart from Christ, we are clearly not the resurrection and the life. But, do we boldly testify that we have resurrection and life through Christ?

Perhaps it is because we are so aware of our sins, our lacks and our imperfections, we are reluctant to declare we are what God declares us to be. We are told to trust and obey. The choice is ours.

By His choice, we are included in the great "I AM". He chose to clothe Himself with us. Jesus prayed to His father that we may be one with Him and with the Father (John 17:20-24)

Reaching Out In Hope

Reaching out to touch the one who gave him life,
    His hand encounters only air.
Hopelessness increases as he reaches
    Desiring a strong hand to be there.

Deep inside, a promise seems to fade
    Why did he think he deserved more?
Some around him seem to have it,
    Could it come, though it's never been before?

Dreams of belonging: gone with awakening,
    Is there hope that he'll survive?

Each day darker as prospects decrease
      That for him light would arrive.

Many substitutes allure him
      To be held, would that be gain?
If not truth, then fantasy calling
      Even brief relief seem better than the pain,

Yet God promised not to leave him
      Solitary, lonely and afraid
Said "He'd place him in a family
      With welcoming hearts already made".

The Everlasting Father sends His Spirit
      Extending arms of love and grace.
Receives the one who reaches toward Him
      His strong hands designed the place.

Lifted from the miry clay, to stand
      With brothers new, receiving blessing
Family units define the Kingdom
      By their love, His love confessing.

He's found, at last, his Heavenly Father
      Clothed in love, by one who cares.
Here the strength and hope he needed
      The Fathers heart in one who shares.

Looking back, the trials look different.

Clearly he had believed a lie.
Eyes, now opened, sees the trap set
    From the destroyer, doomed to die.

Now this one who's found sure footing
    Reaches out with now-strong hand
Extend.

If You Are Thirsty, Come and Drink
John 7: 37-38

The words of Jesus, to those who can hear:
    "Living water from your person shall flow."
After he ascended, He promised He'd send
    The power of His Spirit – we'd know.
        Is our channel ready to go?

As water flows from our inmost being
    Can we make sure it's offered as pure?
Without add or subtracting the life it contains
    Giving freely what was given, for sure?
        Have we been good stewards of the gifts?

Is it pure water, can it nourish life
    Or has it been polluted somehow?
How can its safety be fully known?
It is essential, we need it right now!
    How can we be sure?

Loren's Musings

As the river of life flows on and on
      How can anyone get what he needs?
Is it coming fast from a water-fall
      Or slowly passing through reeds?
          Can anyone really take it?

Our job - to be ready to let the life flow
      Our source has abundant supply.
We'll make it available to ones who have need
      Never forced or made hard to apply
          Can we be a still water place?

Knowing we're not the source, we're glad to be used
      To deliver the water, then rest
Living water, abundant, can flow through ourselves
      The plan of our Lord is the best.
          Only wanting "well done" from our King

Always Something New To Learn

I am always thrilled, amazed and humbled when some word or phrase or picture in God's word is given meaning or illumination that has hitherto been missed by me or others.

Recently I was reading the 22nd Psalm and came to verse six which reads "but I am a worm and no man." Since this Psalm is prophetic of the passion of Jesus on the cross, I had assumed that this was an expression of Jesus' humility. A portion of the commentary by Henry Morris in "The New Defenders Bible casts new light on this expression. He writes, "this same word refers to the worm from which the Israelites of that day obtained their red dyes and is usually translated "crimson" or "scarlet". The female worm of this species, when laying her eggs, affixes her body to a wood surface on which she will die after the young are born. The wood, her body, and the young are reddened with the death of the life-giving mother. In a similar image the Lord Jesus made "peace through the blood of his cross" (Colossians 1:20).

This is such a vivid word picture to me: Jesus giving up his life blood on the cross in order that we may obtain life. I wonder why it has taken so long for this to come to my attention. I have renewed hope that many other things will become clear once they have been brought into some new illumination. It is true, of course, that faith is not dependent upon seeing this kind of explanation. In the same way that we do not have to wait for some archeological find to prove the accuracy of what has been stated in the Word of God.

God does tell us to be aware of the world around us such as: "look at the lilies of the field", "go to the ant and observe", or "does a sparrow fall to the ground unknown to God?" Natural things are used to give a base of understanding so that many levels of lessons may be gained by the contemplation of a story or parable.

The value of a parable is our knowledge of something that we have seen or experienced providing a base for understanding the spiritual (and therefore essential) significance of a matter. Paul explains in I Corinthians 16:46, "the spiritual is not first, but the natural and afterwards the spiritual." If we are familiar with seeds, growing plants, sheep raising, being careful and wise with money, etc; we are then ready to see the eternal or spiritual significance of the example being used.

Since all of Gods' word is given to us for teaching, for reproof, for correction, and for training in righteousness (2 Timothy 2:16), we do not want to miss out on any lessons due to our lack of understanding of the natural base. It is good for us to dig into the word of God and to appreciate what others have previously dug out for our enlightenment. Gods promise to us is that we will be changed by the renewing of our minds (Romans 12:2).

Stillness

There are many states of being which are ours to choose.
One can: Be satisfied. Be joyful. Be disappointed.

None of these requires an action on our part – merely a decision to be.
Myriad states of being can be chosen when given the same set of circumstances.
We have often heard, "Be still and know that I am God."
Here a psalmist leads us to a door of decision. (Psalm 46: 10-11)
We must see this as an invitation – not a command.
The rewards of our decision are stated here.
Should we make this choice?
What defines stillness?
 +Confidence in Gods' purposes
 +Lack of anxiety concerning ones own abilities
 +Openness to be taught and be change
The promises stated here are:
 +Knowing God in His exalted state
  Both among people (nations)
  And over all the earth (universe)
 +Coming into a deeper realization
  That He is, as he has promised, with us
  That He identifies His relationship with mankind as the
  God and Father of Abraham, Isaac, and Jacob;
  A fatherly, generational connection.

+We can further know God as our fortress, our safe place,
   our refuge.
      A place of freedom from fear.

If we choose this place of stillness:
   +We can know God relationally, experientially, securely
When we know God, His heart and His ways
   +We can learn to know ourselves more properly.

Let's respond to the invitation to "Be still and Know"

Control or Release

In the letter to the Ephesians the apostle Paul wrote that the work of the leaders was to equip the saints for the works of service (ministry) for the building up of the Body of Christ.

Paul saw, through the eyes of God, the process of the body becoming more mature and able to speak the truth to those around them about the freedom in Christ available to them to deal with the besetting problems of the world.

Similarly, our desire should be to see others through God's eyes, looking to see His purposes for them and doing our part to equip them for their individual work.

Often, as a parent or a teacher, one finds it easier to concentrate on the boundaries rather than the core of the situation. Building up the foundations is more basic and helpful than external appearances or limits.

However, we have a choice when we are involved with others.

We can inform in order to control and contain them or to equip and encourage them with the view in mind to release them fully to their unique purposes. Rules, regulations, boundaries and protocol all have their place, but these are to be the externals of life together, not the heart of it.

Paul told his disciple Timothy to stir up the gift that was in him to motivate him to do all that was in him so that he would be able to give what he had to others. We must become students of those we would like to motivate toward maturity and fruitfulness.

When we are involved with friends, neighbors, family or strangers, let us consider our actions and our speech so that we are giving what will help the other ones to enter fully into the opportunities given to them.

Let us fully receive the grace of God and give it freely to others.

The choice is ours: inform to control or equip to release.

Eager For The 'New'

There is something in relation to 'new' that is intriguing and compelling.

'New' and 'New and Improved' remain the most used and most effective words in advertising.

Probably what is underlying this effectiveness is that these words give hope for something better than what we already have or what we

have experienced.
However, we have often been disappointed or disillusioned when this hope has not been fulfilled.

It is likely that we have all had desires for something new:

What, for instance, is defined as a new thought?
Would it only apply to my own past thoughts or must it just be the first encounter for me?

Many things do bear the name of new or fresh, like flowers, fruit, or new born babies, even though ones like them have been seen before.

It would be difficult to find something never before seen.
The Bible says that there is nothing new under the sun.

Yet it also says that the steadfast love of the Lord is new every morning land that He will put a New Song in our hearts.
And also, we have the remarkable promise "I will give you a new heart and I will put a New Spirit within you" Ezekiel 36:20

It seems that only what is given by God is actually new.

If this is so, how can I make myself ready to receive the newness of Gods' gifts?

To begin with, I can rid myself of whatever would block my appreciation of the promises that God has clearly made to me. For starters: unbelief and a stiff neck.

Then I can cry out, as King David did "Create in me a clean heart, Oh God, and renew a right Spirit within me."

Whenever I receive something new, I want to be led by His Spirit to steward it properly and share it at the appropriate time with others,

allowing it to be new with them as well.

Solomon – The Wisest One

What does it take for us to learn?
What will it take for us to turn?

One went before us who tried it all out
He wanted to know what life was about.

With money no object, he planned and he built
He withheld no pleasure and he felt no guilt.

Thinking many mates surely are better than one,
Had hundreds of partners before he was done,

Found time for all choices, to hate or to love,
But times are not right without help from above,

Tried his own way to live life, now he knows
That without God all is vapor that instantly goes.

So take heart, my brothers, learn from the past.
The lessons are written, His wisdom will last.

VI. Rites of Passage

God's Man

You are no longer a child. You are now a young man
      Responsibilities come with that place.
You have had privileges, God saw to that:
      He's prepared you to run a good race.

You're unique, you are special, you're one of a kind
      Since you're rare, you have value you know.
Before worlds began, God knew of this day
      He fashioned the way you would grow.

God calls you "His Own," what wonderful truth
      You are "family," He gave you a name
Christ died for our sins so that you can live free
      That's better than riches or fame.

We welcome you to the company of men
      You're a great addition, that's sure
So now "man of God" rise up and stand firm
      Let His word be your guide, clear and pure.

To a Young Man

As you walk down the path God has chosen for you
    There will be many obstacles you will meet
And there will be paths to attract you away
    From those, you will need to retreat.

There will be times that you will want to quit
    But your gift-mix will spur you along
Your love of rhythm and water will help
    But only God will help you stay strong.

It has been said that every man
    Will walk to a different beat
Deep inside you, you will find
    A source that's both pure and sweet

Rely on the fact that you have been chosen
    By God to be a light in the world
To be moved by the wind of the Spirit
    Like a flag that is being unfurled.

As your life is unfolded for all to see
    Many will ask of you "Who is your source?"
You can boldly proclaim in a voice strong and clear
    "He is Jesus, my Savior, of course.

Today You Are a Man

You've always been a male
      But today you are a man
You are on the path of growing up
      According to God's plan.

Ahead of you lie choices
      Your decisions really count
You'll only see when looking back
      How they interlock and mount.

Give attention to the sources
      Of the things that influence you
Are they fleeting or temporary
      Or eternal, tried and true.

Many things and folks will woo you
      Saying life is just a game
But the end of that is sadness
      And you alone must take the blame

The path is yours to choose each day
      And if you strive to know God's best
You can count on Him to give you
      Steps for this day and all the rest.

So today you are a man, my son
      Your future spreads out bright
Now as God's Son, 'Rise Up Oh Man'
      He's prepared you for the fight.

Andrew – Passing The Bar

It may be just a day, but it's a mark along the way
  Going from being a boy to being a man,
Bringing things from chaos into a place of order
  Is the current purpose as you follow God's own plan.

Coming to the masculine side to be mentored now
  To be fitted daily into the maturation mold
Willing to stand and look fear right in the face
  Not desiring retreat, when your blood is running cold.

Knowing, being certain, that your way has been prepared.
  He made you special, He's the one who knows you well.
You are gifted like no other, for His purpose made you fit
  When your tasks are over, we'll see you've done it well.

You now take on stewardship of many jobs and things,
  Standing and shining with the light from His own face
Leading and guiding you with choices every day
  Your decisions will define your future and your place.

Take courage, Drew, stand tall, you are on the right road.
  We all do wish you "God's speed" on your way.
Though none can do it for you, we will be by your side,
  As your manhood will be proven from this day.

Coming Of Age

As you walk down the path God has chosen for you,
There will be many obstacles you will meet
And there will be paths to attract you away
From those, you will need to retreat.

There will be times that you will want to quit,
But your gift-mix will spur you along.
Your love of rhythm and water will help
But only God will help you stay strong.

It has been said that every man
Will walk to a different beat;
Deep inside you, Mathew, you will find
A source that's both pure and sweet.

Rely on the fact that you have been chosen
By God to be a light in this world,
To be moved by the wind of the Spirit
Like a flag that is being unfurled.

As your life is unfolded for all to see
Many will ask of you "Who is your source?"
You can boldly proclaim in a voice strong and clear
"He is Jesus, my Savior, of course".

He's Already Ten

Dear Mathew,

You have traveled for more than a decade on the journey of life. The things that you have learned already will be useful for you, since nothing is wasted. Whether we learn more from our successes or our failures is up to each individual. Everything, except fatalities, can be useful. Many can aid us in avoiding the fatal things.

If you can see yourself through God's eyes or through the eyes of many who care for you, you will do well.

Your given gifts and talents cover a wide range and all need attention and developing. In spite of our usual impatience, all can be attended too, if given the time, proper attention and prayer.

Although your course is unique, for there never has been or ever will be anyone with your same gift mix, there are pitfalls and interesting diversions that you will want to avoid.

1. Following the crowd will be a temptation, but not a good idea.
2. Finding the easiest way is a short-cut that takes the longest time. The path of least resistance makes both men and rivers crooked.
3. Waiting until you feel like it before you tackle a task will allow good paths to be missed with no chance to turn around

Final judgment will be on the basis of what you have done with what you have been given to work with. This mark is different for each individual.

VII. Marriage

Fifty Married Years of Ministry Up North

The northern part of Michigan, under the bridge
    Has certainly been blessed with a treasure.
When the two of you came to live there,
    God's blessings came along without measure.

Too many who came under their loving care,
    They listened, gave and practiced God's grace
As they held out their hands and their hearts
    To all who were hurting who came to their place.

Together we celebrate this union of theirs,
    We think fifty years is a pretty good start.
We look to the future, we're sure there's more fruit
    God's hand moving on as they stick to their part.

So blow horns and whistles and hear a Sven joke
    Celebrating a half century past.
As God planned the beginning and now leads us on
    Believing this union is destined to last.

Life Together

All through the ages, the songs people sing express the state of the heart. Many of the lyrics have been helpful in expressing values and desires and struggles and successes in marriage, viewed as a lifelong friendship.

One pre-world war II song belted out "You're the cream in my coffee, you're the meat in my stew, confidentially, positively, I'd be lost without you." It seemed to express the spark of togetherness and excitement of the combination of two lives working together.

Another song stated "The weather outside is frightful, but inside it's so delightful. As long as I have you, let it snow, let it snow, let it snow." Whatever the circumstances – facing them together is not only bearable but best.

For us, the Kenny Rogers song "Through The Years" captures the continuity and progression of the friendship in our marriage.

I can't remember when you weren't there
When I didn't care for anyone but you
I swear we've been through everything there is
Can't imagine anything we've missed
Can't imagine anything the two of us can't do

Loren's Musings

We have always looked forward to having time together – lunch hour, days off call, evenings after the children were in bed or after they were older, waiting for their return from activities. These precious times were spent making plans, reflecting sharing, reading to each other or just being together.

Some one said that the true test of friendship is to sit or walk with each other for an hour in perfect silence without wearying one another.

Through the years, you've never let me down
You turned my life around, the sweetest days I've found
I've found with you ... Through the years
I've never been afraid, I've loved the life we've made
And I'm so glad I've stayed, right here with you
Through the years

If we didn't have money, we did free things, if we had it we spent it. We were perfectly fulfilled with whatever presented itself, whatever was appropriate.

I can't remember what I used to do
Who I trusted, whom I listened to before.
I swear you've taught me everything I know
Can't imagine needing someone so
But through the years it seems to me
I need you more and more

Loren's Musings

With a true friend, you can bring out your deepest thoughts (some still young and incomplete) and also show your struggles and weaknesses. It is a relief and comfort to know that someone knows you for what you are and still cherishes you; to know you can be honest and not be misunderstood.

Through the years, through all the good and bad
I knew how much we had, I've always been so glad
To be with you ... Through the years

It's better everyday, you've kissed my tears away
As long as it's okay, I'll stay with you
Through the years

Close relationships are hard to manage, but the work of going through the problems together caused them to get better with time. I would add to the lyrics, "I've never been afraid, I've loved the life we've made, I'm so glad I've stayed, - right here with you.

Through the years, when everything went wrong
Together we were strong, I know that I belonged
Right here with you ... Through the years
I never had a doubt, we'd always work things out
I've learned what love's about, by loving you
Through the years

God never promised a life without troubles, but he did say that as he took us through each one that He would never leave us or forsake us. As God has made us one, He is the strongest part of the three-fold-cord which binds us together.

68

Through the years, you've never let me down
You've turned my life around, the sweetest days I've found
I've found with you ... Through the years
It's better everyday, you've kissed my tears away
As long as it's okay, I'll stay with you
Through the years!

Because we each made a vow ("by my own free will, I vow not to quit") we have been able to let out personalities mesh into oneness. For example; in planning an outing, Rea's concerns would be for the practical details while Loren's emphasis would be toward the relational benefits.

Friendship in marriage raises the quality of life above the perfunctory, obligation or duty. A true friend can choose an appropriate activity or a gift at any time, not limited to an expected occasion or holiday. As the word says "A man should dwell with his wife according to his growing understanding of his wife and that a wife should learn to please her own husband." Our lives should be single-minded towards our mate, investing ourselves in enhancing our growing friendship.

From Grandpa to Newly Weds

They have now become one!
    Joyful shouts are heard far and wide.
By the fruit of this union, lives will be touched
    As they walk 'in the Lord' side by side.

For one plus one equals more than two;
    Even engineer's math must agree.
When "Look how they love one another" is said,
    For their heart, by their actions, is easy to see.

Their love for "Lord Jesus" is contagious to all.
    Get close to them and you'll catch it too.
The Lord and His Bride is pictured by them;
    This intimacy is promised to you.

He gives a "New Song" both the notes and the words
    Inviting us all to join in.
This union is promised, get involved in the dance
    Today is the time to begin.

By recalling their past, we have hope for the future.
    Both sides now brighten the day.
We'll continue to pray and wish them Gods' speed
    For now they are married, HOORAY!!!

Sharing Life Together

Lord, your word says "look around and see the natural"
　　So that you can show us the spirit of a thing.
What could possibly be the natural lesson
　　Which could show the value that a friend could bring?

Would it be the silver lining of a dark cloud
　　Preceding the bright sky as the dark clouds go?
Could it be the welcome freshness after the rain
　　Which brings invigoration when one needs it so?

Is it drinking fresh clean water coming from a mountain stream
　　After treading upward thinking, "I will never make it"?
Then, strength comes when a fellow traveler urges onward
　　And you realize, for sure, alone you couldn't take it?

Just as peaceful sleep refreshes after struggles all day long
　　So does fellowship bring energy when your tank is low,
In a place of safety, no denying where you are,
　　Encouraged, once again, life's river starts to flow.

Two or more together, when meeting in His Name,
　　Jesus, by His Spirit, joins and fills all space.
No wonder that our enemy, the liar, tries his best
　　To disconnect us from each other and destroy our face to face.

To share a burden with a friend and see the problem cut in half
　　Or share a joy and have it multiplied is grand.
What a gift from God it is to have a brother
　　How does He do that for us? That is hard to understand.

Loren's Musings

To be sharpened by a brother as you work a common task
        Brings glory to our God, and energy to every man.
When "Well done my faithful servants" is
heard from our Lord's lips
        True joy is multiplied to us as no other statement can.

For each of you, my brothers, I now give thanks to God,
        Who in His grace and mercy, has joined you each to me.
Brothers to love and be loved by, the richest gift by far
        Surrounded by so many fine men, how blessed can one man be?

Made in the USA
Middletown, DE
16 November 2018